12
LESSONS
on
LIFE
I Learned from My Garden

12
LESSONS
on
LIFE
I LEARNED FROM MY
GARDEN

Spiritual Guidance from the Vegetable Patch

BY VIVIAN ELISABETH GLYCK

Daybreak™ Books
A Division of Rodale Press, Inc.
Emmaus, Pennsylvania

Cover and Book Designer: Debra Sfetsios
Cover and Interior Illustrator: Jane Mjølsness

Library of Congress Cataloging-in-Publication Data

Glyck, Vivian Elisabeth.
    12 lessons on life I learned from my garden: spiritual
guidance from the vegetable patch/by Vivian Elisabeth Glyck.
        p.   cm.
    ISBN 0–87596–426–5   hardcover
    1. Christian life. 2. Gardens—Religious aspects—
Christianity. 3. Glyck, Vivian Elisabeth.   I. Title.
BV4501.2.G585 1997
248.4—dc21   96–36844

Distributed in the book trade by St. Martin's Press

2 4 6 8 10 9 7 5 3 1 hardcover

---- OUR PURPOSE ----

*"We publish books that empower
people's minds and spirits."*

For my mother, Myrta Weiss Glyck, whose

wisdom sneaks up on me when I least expect

it. Your constancy and nonjudgment have

made me so brave.

Contents

A C K N O W L E D G M E N T S

Love and thanks to: Deepak Chopra, who taught me the true meaning of "infinite possibilities"; my brother Gordon for always keeping my foot on the gas; my brother Julian for his subtle support; my dear friend Arthur Ivey for the generosity of his "quiet space" in which I wrote this book; Masha Alexander and Lynn Franklin for their enthusiasm and guidance; Karen Kelly for "getting" my vision; Janet Bar-David for seeing me more clearly than I see myself; Tony Martinelli, Jr., for the "technical" advice that gave life to my metaphors; Jim Martinelli for learning so many lessons with me; and my beautiful niece and nephews, Allison, Daniel, Brandon, and Eric, who are perfect illustrations of how magnificently things grow when nurtured with love.

"Every natural fact is a

symbol of some spiritual fact."

RALPH WALDO EMERSON

INTRODUCTION

Sometimes it's amazing how something so simple can come along, and in the split second it takes to change a perception, your life is irrevocably altered. That's how it happened with me and my garden.

For many years I had been the lazy woman's gardener. In my usual Tom Sawyer way, I would rally as many friends as I could to help me plow my lot. I ended up having a garden abundant with the usual fare of zucchini, peppers, lettuce, tomatoes, and eggplant—a veritable ratatouille of sorts with very little effort on my part.

But beginning several years back, something deep inside me said, "Do it yourself. Don't take a shortcut. It'll be more satisfying that way."

So against my better judgment (and against my manicurist's advice), that is just what I did.

Now, plenty of other things urged me along in this direction. For the first time in my life, I had been meditating on a regular basis. I refused to meditate in some dark, secluded room. Rather, I always searched for a brilliant natural setting that would embrace me and my techno-weary spirit: on the top of a snow-covered mountain in winter, on a carpet of pine needles in a clearing by a babbling brook in the spring, or just out in my wooded back-yard in the summer.

The closer my spirit and I got to nature, the clearer the somewhat-fuzzy connection between spirit and nature became. Perhaps Ralph Waldo Emerson said it best in his essay entitled *Nature*: "The greatest delight which the fields and woods minister is the suggestion of an occult relation between man and the vegetable."

I like to put it a bit more simply: Nature—she's a smart cookie. She knew long before the wheel was ever invented not to reinvent the wheel. There is a reason for the correlation between our inner voice and the calamities that befall us when we don't listen to that voice. (Just think about the relationship you knew that you should have gotten out of years ago, or the job whose demands and improprieties violated your true nature but you stuck with because, after all, it meant security.)

I know you'll forgive the triteness, but it is true: We are one with nature. The wonder of the universe is within us. It's not something we observe and then ignore as we overlook a brilliant purple sunset in our high-speed chase to get to the meeting, swallow our opinions to make the boss happy, and generally behave like the short-sighted scholars who need proof that nature, mind, body, and spirit suffer when they are separated from each other.

So, my little book is about listening and reacting to the cues that nature gives us. Growing my garden, I've realized that everything is about relationships. I've witnessed that ultimately you can't take what you don't give because there is a master bookkeeper out there who keeps accounts balanced. This fundamental link between man, plants, and the earth has been documented since the dawn of civilization. That's why whenever I'm particularly frustrated by a problem in my life or in my garden, I meditate on the words of Saint Paul in his letter to the Galatians, "Be not deceived; God is not mocked: for whatsoever a man soweth, that shall he also reap."

"The Book of Life begins with

a man and a woman in

a garden."

OSCAR WILDE

PREPARATION IS EVERYTHING

1

If you don't start with a good foundation, your growth will flounder.

Having grown up on the Upper West Side of New York City (in a tenement of sorts), I didn't have a very strong relationship with nature. On special days my mother would bundle up my brothers and me and shepherd us happily off to Riverside Drive, a park that is bordered by the West Side Highway and the Hudson River. There, we would gingerly step past the sleeping homeless people and the empty Thunderbird wine bottles to nestle ourselves in a cozy spot by the banks of the then extremely polluted Hudson. With zeal that only children have, we would dig at the earth for hours on end, piling up unfortunate earthworms on which we would perform ruthless surgery.

It never ceased to amaze me that I could cut these worms into little parts and they would continue to squirm with life. My brothers told me that it was because they had sixteen hearts, one in every section of their little bodies. I still don't know if that's true, but at the time I believed everything my brothers had to say. Earthworm experiments on Riverside Drive were the closest contact with nature that my parents could provide me in my young life.

My parents had more important things on their minds. Immigrants from the former Yugoslavia, they were pretty intent on finding a few dollars for the next meal, figuring out how to get their precocious offspring into private schools without shelling out a year's income, and sheltering us from the frightening population that congregated around the liquor store downstairs.

So when I grew up and finally bought my own little acre in the 'burbs, I was faced with quite a predicament. I knew when I was house hunting that a garden was going to be one of my efforts in fashioning a bond with the cosmos. Therefore, it was a priority that I had space and sun. After everything else was unpacked, I bought a shovel, a gardening book, and a pair of gloves and headed out for the sunniest spot I could find.

There, in my usual cutting-corners way, I turned the soil over once, added a little bit of manure, and stuck a few tomato plants and zucchini seeds into the ground.

They didn't do too badly, mind you, but they certainly didn't flourish. The tomatoes grew to a decent size and ripened well enough for me to create some salsa. But it certainly wasn't a bumper crop that had me opening a roadside stand just to get rid of the surplus.

The zucchini did okay, too. The plants started off with a great show. Big, edible yellow blossoms captured the attention of every yellow jacket and bumblebee within a two-mile radius. But the yield was disappointing. First, the flowers began to wilt and the fruit that followed didn't quite take. They grew a few inches and then rotted on the vine. Little did I know at the time that everyone (except for me) knows how to grow zucchini. And the rumors that I heard about gardeners harvesting such great quantities of zucchini that they stooped to leaving mammoth-size gourds on the back porches of neighbors at night certainly was not a fate to befall me.

So, after my first season in the garden, I did my homework. I talked to every local farmer who would give me the time of day. I grilled them for information. What I found out was really quite simple: If you don't start with a good foundation, your growth will flounder.

Soon, I adopted a successful tomato farmer, Tom Hanson, whose farm was about ten miles from my house. Many a Saturday in the summer I would rise at 6:00 A.M. and rummage around my garden with anxiety. Something was eating my tomatoes; they weren't growing with a healthy flourish. The onions weren't taking. The yellow squash were progressing at a snail's pace.

Weary with my seeming failures, I would pile my sad harvest into a plastic bag, throw it on the back of my bike and pedal uphill to the Hanson farm. As I crested the hill, the silence and beauty of the back-country road would engulf me. The higher I climbed, the more I could see of Tom's beautiful, verdant farm.

Heaving with the effort, I would stumble into his little stand. As I guzzled water, Tom would examine the samples I brought and reassure me about my feeble attempts at cultivation. He encouraged me to test the soil: Was it too acidic or too alkaline? (He guessed it was too acidic, considering my neck of the woods.) Then he told me to dig deep, to really turn up the soil, and to study it. He persuaded me to find out what it needed, add lime, feed it frequently with nutrients, and add back what nature—through wind, winter, and water—had taken out.

And wouldn't you know that the very next year, I was the desperate neighbor, eager to share my bounty with anyone who didn't hide when they saw me coming with all the big green and yellow zucchini under my arm.

But the lesson for me was quite haunting. I thought, and still do to this day, how preparation, or more often lack thereof, has impacted my life. How many times my attempts at relationships, work, or recreation have suffered because of my cursory approach to them. And how rewarding and fruitful it has been for me when I invest my time, energy, and love into the things that are important to me.

Building a sound foundation is hard work. And I still look to my garden when I forget my lesson. So many times I have blamed my potential life partners for not being perfect when in fact it has been me who hasn't made the commitment, who hasn't taken the time to get to know who they are before I make big demands of the relationship. I rely on my expectations and dreams to provide the foundation on which I build my goals. Then, of course, I'm disappointed when I don't harvest the perfect relationship in no time at all.

On the other hand, the most fruitful love, sex, and intimacy that I've ever had has been that which I've yielded after learning what my partner needed, after digging deep both within him and me to bring to the surface the richest aspects of us both. And when there was a deficit of some kind, I added love, support, and encouragement instead of concentrating on the outcome I wanted. Now sometimes, our resulting creation was just a bad seed no matter what. But most of the time, it grew without effort, sparkled with life, and was as strong as the season would allow.

Stay focused on how to best serve the present by keeping your foundation strong, and the future ultimately will prosper.

"Our bodies are our gardens,

to the which our wills

are gardeners."

WILLIAM SHAKESPEARE

2

Follow the wisdom provided by nature.
Everything in moderation—sunlight, water,
nutrients. Too much of a good thing will topple
your structure.

The very essence of nature is harmony
and balance. A plant always grows
upward—toward the light. Just look at an oak tree.
The lower branches reach out farther than the ones

above, providing strength and equilibrium for the entire tree. The tree is naturally constructed to brave the harsh climate of wind and weather where it grows.

In my garden, after I worked hard to test my soil and correct the level of acidity versus alkalinity, I would watch as nature balanced herself through the elements. Many days of scorching sun and heat would go by, and the only rest that my poor plants would get was the cool of the evening. The elements still took their toll on my fledgling eggplants and peppers, even though I would water them daily.

Every day I would come home and rush to their side, as my plants drooped wearily and a gasp of wind fluttered through their limp leaves. I would observe in wonder as the heat turned into a rich thunderstorm, which doused more water and cooling than I could ever hope to offer.

And then a cloudy day or two would roll in and rescue my crop. It was a beautiful dance between my garden and the sky. Sometimes on the verge of tragedy, sometimes in joy and ecstasy, but always in balance like two old friends who know the score but love to rehearse their parts over and over.

I felt like a silent observer, privileged to watch, and at some cosmic level I knew I was there to play a very real role in their dance. I was like a gentle referee who knew when a bad call was being made and when to step in to add my own weight to keep the balance perfect.

As it is for my garden, balance has been an ongoing struggle for me. In my closest intimate relationships I've labored between giving too much and taking too much. I find that when I give too much, I don't have enough left for myself. When I take more, my partner is left depleted.

Sometimes I, too, droop with the effort of maintaining balance, but then I receive a good dousing of support and affection and have the strength to return love. When one of us needs more than the other for too long, the balance is thrown off and growth is halted for a time. As long as we can keep growing toward the light, we flourish. It is a constant push and pull that allows us to achieve the synergy that we need to grow strong.

I think that achieving balance in all of life is the challenge of our times. So many of my friends juggle work, family, community, exercise, relationships, and self-growth. When things topple, it always seems to be in the area of personal growth. When balance is thrown askew, just like in the garden, all areas of life suffer.

I see my newfound knowledge of myself or spirituality as the center of my balance. When I don't find a brief time to be in silence each day, my equilibrium is thrown off. I don't take good care of myself. My exercise and diet fall off. My ability to generate love and compassion for others is diminished. And I lose the power of perspective only to become embroiled in the endless ego battles that beckon me from all corners of my life.

It's only when I can find my center through things that are truly important to me, like reading, traveling, self-knowledge, and meditation, that I can silence the mindless conversation of my ego and come home to who I truly am.

Like the oak tree, find balance at your center, and all of the branches of your life will grow in harmony to support the structure of who you really are.

"If the single man plants

himself indomitably on his

instincts, and there abides,

the huge world will come

round to him."

RALPH WALDO EMERSON

PATIENCE IS A VIRTUE

3

You can't harvest what you don't sow. So plant your desires, gently nurture them, and they will be rewarded with abundance.

Every vegetable gardener wants things to grow faster. Throughout time, we have contrived any number of ways to fertilize, water, and cultivate to get an earlier yield. But, no matter how much wishing and effort goes into it, I've never seen a plant in a hurry.

My garden grows in its own good time. Every plant has its season. Lettuce comes up early and must be picked or else it will bolt. Kale gets planted late in the season because it loves the cool weather of fall. Asparagus takes years to prosper, and strawberries can take up to two seasons to provide a harvest. Frost-sensitive crops like tomatoes, peppers, cucumbers, and zucchini love the sweltering, sultry heat of the depths of summer, when they propagate so passionately that the bees can barely keep up.

Even though I know all of this, sometimes I can't wait to find out what's going to happen next. Many times I've been tempted to go out to my little mound of dirt where I've recently planted yellow squash and poke beneath the earth to see how the seed is growing. In the same way, it's so tempting to disturb those zealous, overachieving radishes, which thrust their sprouts above the ground in no time at all, just to see if the root is growing below ground as quickly as the plant grows above.

When a season goes poorly for a crop, I'm impatient and frustrated. I blame myself for my slovenly gardening habits, certain that I have played a very real role in the demise of the brussels sprouts. And I know that I am responsible for the paltry production of the snap peas because I didn't provide the right trellis.

It's not until the next season, the next year, that I am able to acknowledge the lessons that I have absorbed. Ultimately, the insight that I have gained from my pain and failures has made me a better gardener than I could have hoped to become from the most studious preparation.

Patience is perhaps the most profound lesson I have learned from my garden. I used to struggle to control every aspect of my life. From my family to my career to my relationships, I knew how to make things happen. I knew that if I held on and mastered and controlled, I could succeed in having things go my way.

The times I have worked hardest to gain control

are when I have felt lost in life. When I wanted to start my own business, I felt frightened and insecure. I fought so hard to find a solution that I just ended up becoming more lost. I fretted about everything. Would I have enough to keep me busy? Would I be lonely working by myself? Most of all, how was I going to make a living? Popular wisdom told me that I needed a couple of solid commitments from clients before I could quit my job. I had no ability to just be in the moment and let things unfold. That was when my friend Debbie said to me, "Look at yourself, Vivian. You're so powerful, you can't help but succeed. You're not trusting in the universe. Just put it out there and trust."

And so I did. I listened closely to my intuitive voice about what I ultimately wanted and sowed the seeds of my desires. Then I stood still, knowing that I had prepared my foundation as best I could. It was time to be patient and wait for what would emerge. Just like I learned to do with my garden, I stopped hovering nervously over what I had cultivated and allowed myself to be in the discomfort of not knowing what was going to happen next (as though I ever did).

What sprang forth was extraordinary. With very little effort I closed on two substantial contracts that would sustain me in my new business, my good friend Bill set up a new computer system for me, and the phone started ringing off the hook with new potential business. I got everything I wanted by doing nothing at all.

Being in the moment and giving up control of the future takes discipline. I have learned to sow my most cherished longings and wait for them to bloom. Although I am tempted to dig them up to see how they're growing, most often I refrain. When I do tinker around with the growth by trying to control the outcome of things, by managing the process too tightly, I mess everything up. Now, if I want something, like more money, new friends, to hear from someone in particular, or for my relationships to be better, I put forth the intention and then wait for things to unfold. It's nothing short of miraculous how I get what I want by patiently waiting for things to come to me, and I would have told anyone he was loony if I hadn't experienced it for myself.

Standing still, doing nothing, waiting for our desires to come to us is the most difficult lesson to learn in this go-get-'em society. But when I follow the advice given to me by nature, I know that I can't go wrong.

> *Follow your intuition, plant your desires, stand still, be patient. The universe will provide bounty, the likes of which you can only dream.*

"The finest qualities of our nature,

like the bloom on fruits,

can be preserved only by the most

delicate handling."

HENRY DAVID THOREAU

CULTIVATE DIVERSITY

4

*Plants, just like people, have their own individual
needs. If you impose your own desires on them, it
will violate their true natures and they will suffer
and die. Accept and nourish their individuality,
and your support will nurture them.*

I can't count the number of years I antici-
pated the last frost of the season by
exhuming my shorts and T-shirt from winter storage

and conducting my annual pilgrimage to the local nursery. There, I overpurchased, as usual, a wide array of seeds, seedlings, fertilizer, lime, peat moss, and an indulgence of updated garden tools.

Back at my plot, I studiously prepared my soil for the soon-to-arrive inhabitants. Just before Memorial Day, which is barely the cusp of the projected final frost in my area, everything went into the ground. The carrot seeds, herbs, eggplant, brussels sprouts, lettuce, strawberries, tomatoes, and zucchini all got planted on the same day.

I was also innocently oblivious as to where I should plant each crop. I knew there were various spots in my garden that received more sun than others. Other spots, although never completely shady, didn't receive the full summer sun throughout the day. You can guess the outcome. Some plants did terrifically; others, like lettuce, which bolted in the full summer sun, and broccoli, which flowered, just embarrassed and frustrated me.

Sometimes, though, it amazed me that no matter what I did to the soil, I could put an itty-bitty seed into the ground, and three months later I would see a brilliant orange carrot top peaking out from below the surface of the soil. How did that tiny seed know to make itself a nutritious carrot? How could so much intelligence be captured in so small a space?

I'll leave the answers to these questions to the scientists and the sages. What I have solved, however, is my role in cultivating the diversity of my plants. If I put that little carrot seed in a hot, sunny spot at the same time that I sow the rest of my would-be vegetables and if I fertilize my carrot the same way I feed the rest of the garden, what I will reap is a small, mangy, fibrous octopus of a carrot with roots that have forked out in every direction.

But, I have a choice. By taking the time to understand that carrot's true nature, I can assist it in becoming the best carrot its little DNA will allow it to be. If I plant it well before the last frost, in a partially shaded area so that it is protected from the heat of the summer sun, and if I feed it less manure and more wood ash since it's a root crop, chances are that I am making a major contribution to helping that carrot realize its full potential.

I think that people are very much like plants in this way. Just as plants need the basics of soil, water, and sun to survive, we need the basics of food, shelter, and love to even make a go of it. But once these needs are dealt with, I think we owe it to ourselves to explore the diversity within us. What special nutrient and care do we need to grow into what we are destined to become? And, moreover, how can we nurture our relationships in such a way that we allow those close to us to mature into their highest forms?

My garden's lesson on cultivating diversity taught me a great deal about management within organizations. As a department head in a company within a relatively conservative industry, I had the opportunity to witness a whole population of employees treated identically. They came into the company, were told what their benefits were, how to dress, when to show up for work, and when to leave. They went through similar training programs and had relatively little flexibility in their work styles.

Fortunately, I was in the marketing communications, or advertising, section of the organization. Although I received a great deal of grief for it, my close-knit team of copywriters and graphic designers were known as the creative types. My graphic design studio was called the Arts and Crafts room, and I delighted in the laughter that emanated from the studio and the increasingly bodacious style of dress in which my designers indulged.

I observed my staff very closely for the particular talents each exhibited, and if their talents didn't exactly match their job descriptions, I did what I could to create a need for their uniqueness and fashion the job around them. I harvested great bounty from this approach, and to this day, my ability to cultivate diversity within my work team is one of the most gleeful aspects of my life.

I've watched a young, meek copywriter who lacked confidence and decisiveness grow into an assertive, talented communicator. Not only did her manner change, but her entire appearance transformed when she was allowed to create her own focus within her job. I've seen a hardworking, yet somewhat burned-out communications maven spring back to life when she was allowed to incorporate her passion for human resources into her daily responsibilities.

Of course, it was not always that easy. I had one employee in particular who, for lack of a better analogy, really wanted to be a carrot when, in fact, she was a radish. Her talents lay so clearly in another direction than the one in which she wanted to go that all I could do was encourage her and let her discover the strength of her true nature. I had another staff member whose unique talents just did not fit in with the needs of the organization. It was like trying to grow tropical fruit in the mean, short summers of New England. She could only grow so far and was constantly frustrated in her attempts to move beyond what the environment would allow her, and so she finally moved on to her own fertile ground.

Although her move was painful for me at the time, I soon recognized the lesson that my garden had taught me long ago.

If you violate the true nature of individuals, they will suffer and in some ways die. Accept and nourish individuality in yourself and others, and you will harvest a rich gathering of talent and stimulation.

"May I a small house and large

garden have;

And a few friends, and many

books, both true,

Both wise, and both delightful too!"

ABRAHAM COWLEY

SOMETIMES LESS IS MORE

5

Prune and cut back on excess, and growth will flourish.

Any patient nursery owner will tell you that the most difficult task for their customers to undertake is the simple maintenance chore of pruning. Faced with pruning, the Sunday gardener is fearful of making a mistake, doesn't want to risk the bushiness and bounty of his crops, and generally shies away from this essential component of good gardening.

I'm not exempt from this fear. Many a tomato plant of mine has nearly toppled in excess, with suckers shooting out in all directions and growing so tall that I couldn't possibly find a stake long enough to support its fragile frame.

The ideal tomato gardener will courageously snip off the suckers that grow in the angle between the leafstalks and the main stem and distract a plant from growing tall. Then when the plant has reached ideal height, he will prune off the ensuing vertical growth so that the fruit on the vine can benefit from the energy that otherwise would go into producing more leaf.

Since I've started gardening and developed the fortitude to prune, it's become much more apparent to me how less is more. When I cut back on excess, growth abounds.

Very poignantly at times, I have experienced the wild distraction that too much fullness in my life brings. I had spent a stretch of many months totally occupied with traveling, making plans, working, exercising, starting a new business on the side, vacationing, staying on top of my social agenda, and so forth. Then I woke up one day to realize that I had many branches in my life, growing indiscriminately and aggressively in every direction. The center of my being was suffering and anemic because I was expending so much energy to feed the chaos.

What brought this home to me on that particular day was when my seven-year-old nephew told me over the phone, "Mommy's mad at you. You never remember anyone's birthday." Out of the mouths of babes, huh? He was right.

While I was occupied to the point of exhaustion, pursuing every avenue possible, I had lost the energy to cultivate the areas of my life that most nourish me. The children in my life are truly the apples of my eye, and the joy that shimmers in them when they are loved beams me back to my essential spirit. The very simplicity of life is its essential beauty, and the more we decorate the tree of our lives with acquisitions and accomplishments at the expense of our neighbors' egos, the more we rob ourselves of our own clarity.

Pruning in my life, just like in my garden, is a constant exercise. I always threaten to bud in a thousand different directions, and sometimes I do because I'm addicted to the whirlwind of activity.

Being in the frenzy of unchanneled growth allows me to avoid the dark side of my being. It gives me permission to ignore my fears of intimacy and to avoid the fact that I am still learning how to truly nourish my spirit so that I may give of my orchard to others.

Life is too short to be consumed by the "doing" of a million inconsequential things that we'll never remember we have completed a year from now.

As hard as it is, when life starts growing wildly in every direction, get out those shears and skillfully snip away the excess that robs your spirit of essential growth.

"We are stardust,

We are golden,

And we've got to get ourselves

Back to the garden."

JONI MITCHELL

TRANSPLANTS TAKE TIME

6

Setting down roots in a new place can seem to threaten our survival. But given enough time, it usually allows us more room to expand.

There comes a time during the season of a vegetable garden's growth when the urgency of summer's call to propagate causes seedlings and plants to begin to crowd themselves.

For the novice gardener like me, this causes stress and tension because it means that I must make new room. I must decide which seedlings get to stay, which to thin and discard for the benefit of all concerned, and which to uproot and transplant.

It's a bit disheartening to interfere with the unbridled growth that takes place almost in front of my eyes. The zucchini grow in such surreal haste that I now know where inspiration for *Invasion of the Body Snatchers* came from. The new, delicate, green, lacy plumage of the carrots dances in the breeze of their partly shady neighborhood, and the five varieties of tomatoes I overzealously plant fight with each other for the sun that they need to help me maintain my reputation for creating the best Puttanesca sauce in Massachusetts.

It's tempting to just watch without disrupting this silent fiesta in my backyard. But my parental concern takes over, and I know that if I don't meddle and introduce some discipline, all might be lost.

So, out into the garden I venture with my heart in my mouth and my spade in my hand. As I pull at the large, loping leaves of the zucchini, the plant unwillingly releases the embrace of its neighbor, the summer squash. The entwined limbs of my plum tomatoes threaten to rip as I coax them away from each other. Gently, I unearth their young roots and place my plants in their newly prepared, fresh beds that they will call home for the summer.

In the ensuing days, no matter how much I water or how much I fuss over them, my transplants accusingly droop with listlessness. They behave like punished adolescents in rebellious depression. Anxiously, I review all of my gardening material. Yes, I prepared the ground by mixing together a tantalizing recipe of bonemeal, manure, and a sprinkling of peat moss.

Just when I think that I've made some grievous error, that my plants are destined to die, I come home from work only to find them basking in the sun, firm with turgor, and swaying in bliss. And it just underscores for me how transplants take time.

The first time I attempted transplants in my garden, I had just started a new job. I had been at my previous job for nearly six years. At that old job I knew the ropes, understood and accepted the politics, and had friends who knew my moods, my birthday, my boyfriends, and my work style—but I knew it was time for me to move on.

So, I uprooted myself and plunged into the unknown of my new job. Initially, the move was fraught with difficulty. The personalities and culture were vastly different than what I had known. In a short time I got sick, had confrontations, missed my friends, and generally was totally and completely miserable. I couldn't believe the mistake that I had made. I longed to go back to the security of my old job.

I writhed in unhappiness and discontent. No one understood me. My talents went unrecognized. Many sleepless nights passed, and I convinced myself that I had to do something.

Then one day—and I admit I don't know what day that was or why it happened—I was happy. I knew what I could expect at my new job. I was making inroads and creating new friends. I had gained the confidence of my bosses. I felt as though I was making a difference, and it was apparent in my performance.

And just like my tomato plants that had struggled at first, I, too, had taken root. Through natural course, my soul, my spirit, and my intellect had dug into the new environment and had conspired to get me the nutrients I needed for survival: friends, challenge, recognition, even a new place to have lunch every day. The struggle for creating a livelihood was behind me. I could now move on to my next level of actualization where I could grow, contribute, and realize the fruits of my labor.

My little lesson on transplants, and how they take time, made me think of the many friends I have seen agonize through divorce, move to new cities, change careers, or just move into new homes. The severity of the uprooting varies according to the scenario, but the course of events is always the same.

It begins with great anticipation, then preparation, then physical change, a period of great angst and uncertainty, and, finally, an adaptation and general healthy flourishing of human spirit.

> We are just as sturdy and adaptive as plants. Make the "transplants" you need to in life and trust in your innate ability to thrive.

"Unused capacities atrophy,

cease to be."

T I L L I E   O L S E N

DON'T STAY IN ONE PLACE TOO LONG

If year after year you plant the same vegetables in the same place and don't rotate your crops, your harvest will prove to you the error of your ways. Disease will abound, nutrients once there will have been exhausted by past crops, and the fruits of your labor will be shadows of those past.

Being the novice gardener, I had no idea about crop rotation. But it didn't take too many seasons for me to find out. My vegetable garden is roughly a 20- by 20-foot plot. The southeast corner receives the most sun, while the northwest corner gets only a few hours of sun, even during the longest days of the year. The second year of my garden, I dutifully planted all of my vegetables in exactly the same place that they had been the year before. The vegetables had done okay, so I figured that they were well-placed in terms of sun and irrigation.

I was in for quite a surprise. Nearly everything did poorly (not devoid of production, but just "eh"). There was lots of mold on my zucchini, the tomatoes developed blossom-end rot, and the leaves of my pepper plants were nearly consumed by some dastardly bug. I was thoroughly puzzled. I had heard about crop rotation, but I thought that was something that the big commercial growers had to worry about, not me in my little plot.

So I did some research only to find that every type of gardener—from commercial to domestic— needs to practice the principles of crop rotation. The reasons are really quite simple. First, if crops are properly rotated, the diseases and insects that plague a particular plant one summer and then lie in wait in the soil over the winter will be disappointed not to find the same plant that gave them sustenance the previous year. The parasites will eventually peter out. Second, crops vary in their nutritional needs and therefore deplete the soil in different ways. So, if you plant the same crop in the same place year after year, the soil will be unable to provide the plant with what it needs. Although you can correct some of the problems by adding fertilizer and organic matter, it just doesn't seem to do the job entirely.

This concept has profound implications for me personally. During my career, I had spent many years working for one company. I had great experiences there, but each year the challenges seemed fewer, and the chemistry between my colleagues, my superiors, and myself seemed less dynamic. In fact, one day I realized that as creative and energetic as I had thought I was, I discovered that colleagues perceived me as the "old dog" who probably couldn't learn too many new tricks. But still I held on, trying to protect my territory, hoping that things would change.

Soon my spirit flagged. I developed resentments about how much money other people were making and how they were being treated. I became ensnared in big, ugly political battles. While I was still productive enough to get the job done, I certainly wasn't flourishing. My creativity and leadership were suffering, and I didn't feel as capable as I once had. In fact, I was rotting on the vine. My staff caught some of the disease, too, and followed their leader into blasé cynicism.

It's strange how hindsight is always 20/20. At the time, my perception was that the whole mess was the worst thing that could happen. I felt like a failure. Somehow I hadn't proven to everyone how infinitely valuable I was, how no one else could provide the leadership and creativity of which I was capable. Now I know that it was about what was wrong *for* me, not what was wrong *with* me. I had already absorbed all of the juicy stuff, completed all of the most dynamic projects, learned as much as I could about the business. There was nothing left there to feed me. I had to move on to find new creative sustenance—a fresh soil in which I would thrive.

I wish that I could share the crop rotation metaphor in a way that my closest friends could understand. I see the need to rotate their spirits in their demeanor every day. They seem to be literally devoid of oxygen, with faces gray and listless. They remain attached to jobs and relationships that have fed them well along the way but are now exhausted of the fertile, disease-free nutrients that they need to continue growing. They hold on for dear life, afraid that they'll never find the same security again. What they don't realize is that they have learned to survive on far less than they need in order to realize their full potential. When they do pick up and move, their growth is immediately exponential. The lights turn on in their eyes, there is the undeniable excitement about every day that no one should be without. And when that change is a result of something I may have urged them into, I feel like the most brilliant gardener of all time.

Detach yourself from circumstances that no longer sustain you. Surround your life with fresh thoughts, new challenges, nourishing relationships and fresh knowledge.
Otherwise, your growth will stagnate and eventually draw to a halt.

"Eden is that old-fashioned house

We dwell in everyday

Without suspecting our abode

Until we drive away."

EMILY DICKINSON

ELIMINATE PARASITES

8

Many things love to come and live off your plants, including bacteria, bugs, birds, and bunnies. If you don't control them, entire crops can be ruined. The result of your careful cultivation, in your garden and in your life, can be lost to predators in a short time.

The dog days of summer are pure bliss in my garden. No matter how lousy a gardener I have been that season, there comes a point when everything seems to bloom. I wade into the lushness of tomato plants that tickle my waist, step gingerly over the massive cucumber leaves that have grown big enough to protect their fruit from the harsh summer rays, and stoop to inspect the many varieties of peppers that are growing vigorously.

One day, not so long ago, I came home from work, stepped out of my car, and headed straight for the garden, only to be faced with the horror that every sunny-day gardener has encountered at one time or another. There before me lay the decimation of my efforts. Every lettuce head was gone, gnawed right to the ground. Several peppers lay half-eaten on the ground, and at least five of my largest, juiciest tomatoes hung mortally wounded, bleeding seeds and juice out of their once-firm torsos.

I don't think there is a more maddening, hopeless, helpless feeling. Much of my summer toil was devastated in one short day by some nameless, faceless marauder who had sauntered into my backyard for an afternoon morsel.

The next day, the fence went up. Installed 2 feet

underground and $3\frac{1}{2}$ feet above, my new fence was my statement to the animal kingdom that I intended to protect my assets. That seemed to take care of the lettuce-eaters, but I was still coming home to tomatoes that were partially eaten and damaged beyond salvation.

More frustrated than ever, I stood sentry by my window, awaiting the arrival of my enemy. Soon enough, along came a group of neighborhood crows, eyeing my tomatoes like some sinister gang that wouldn't take no for an answer. Of course, I flew out my door in a rage that sent them scattering in every direction. That was when I got the scarecrow, the mesh netting, and the bright yellow, one-eyed balloon that claimed to be the solution to my bird problem.

But birds and bunnies are nothing compared to the predators and parasites that we face each day. We spend countless dollars on elaborate personal and home security systems and fences to keep ourselves safe from external dangers. Rarely do we realize that most often the real dangers lie within us. It's the internal demons, addictions, and obsessions that flourish inside so many of us, robbing us of our essential nature and the wealth that we have worked so hard to gather within.

This is an addicted society, and many times we become prey to the beasts that inhabit our psyches. As a drug category, antidepressants rank number three of all prescriptions written; $2.9 billion is spent on them annually in this country. That means there are a lot of us who struggle with our internal darkness. I watched my father, a brilliant and passionate man with a zest for life, as he was destroyed by alcohol and barbiturates. Like so many of us, he faced a huge internal void, brought on by self-doubt and lack of self-esteem, which he tried desperately to fill. Maybe I'm being too simplistic, but I don't think he ever realized that by encapsulating himself in the love that was so readily available to him, he could have constructed a fortress around himself, allowing him to salvage his physical and mental health. It seemed so ironic that he invested so much in his own education and growth, but he allowed these predators to deplete him of his rich assets.

Maybe my experience with my father is what set me up to fall in love with men for their "potential." I can't help but shake my head at the literal loss of spirit and life that I have seen when people I love can't seem to eliminate the freeloaders from their lives. As kind and gentle and intelligent as they may be, their efforts at cultivating their characters are lost to the ravenous appetite of their dependencies.

The Bible says that we were turned out from the Garden of Eden when we lost our innocence. I believe that the loss of innocence that happens so early in our lives, the loss of ecstasy, is what we try so desperately to replace. When we lose the childlike ability to shriek with unrestrained laughter or learn to feel self-conscious about how we appear, it is because our egos and vulnerability have moved in where pure observation and naïveté once lived. This loss of innocence leaves us exposed and defenseless (remember how Adam and Eve became aware of their nakedness) and sets up the paradox of forces within us that we will grapple with throughout our lives.

I like to think that if we can fortify our children with a strong enough sense of themselves and a good dose of unconditional love, they will construct their own defenses when toxins threaten their life force. Meanwhile, it's up to us as individuals to maintain and build the self-esteem and self-love that keep us safe from the toxic stuff that surrounds us every day.

Take a look at your life, what toxic relationships, substances and emotions are feeding on your energy and taking away from what you have to give to others. Eliminate them.

"Well we all need someone

we can lean on,

And if you want it,

well you can lean on me."

M I C K   J A G G E R   A N D

K E I T H   R I C H A R D S

Support the Things
You Love

9

Ever try leaving your tomato plants unstaked?
Sometimes it works, but mostly they slither all
over the ground, the fruit decays, and is prey to
disease and furry friends. When you lovingly
stake them and gently tie some rope around
their delicate frames, they flourish and
extend up to the sky.

I love to cook. I'm not sure why. Maybe it's because cooking is one of those activities that commands the attention of all of the senses. The colors, smells, and tastes of the earth's bounty; the wonderful alchemy of heat that transforms food into a meal; and the happy role I play when I add my own touch makes the whole operation quite seductive.

In the summer very little gives me more pleasure than rummaging through my garden for that night's dinner. Snipping off fresh oregano; collecting handfuls of plum tomatoes and 'Big Boys'; and prying off regal eggplants from their stems, while ruminating about what I'm going to do with all of it, is pure joy. Having a couple of happy customers in my kitchen awaiting my creation just adds to the bliss.

I guess it's my love of cooking that makes me feel so passionate about my plum tomatoes. Once, in a moment of irrepressible curiosity, I plucked off a little yellow tomato flower to peer at the itty-bitty promise of fruit behind it. It took my breath away when I saw that the little green swelling behind the flower, smaller than a match head, was actually plum-shaped—a harbinger of things to come. My deep appreciation for this meaty, neat fruit that gives its life to create great sauce is why I become so frustrated and disappointed when things don't go well with my 'Roma' variety.

Several summers back, I took the advice of a favorite gardening book and didn't stake this determinate variety of tomato. One of the problems with determinate tomatoes is that they come up all at once. If you're not ready for them, all of a sudden you have a sizable harvest, literally rotting on the vine. But if you're prepared, you're going to have every kind of sauce stored in the freezer, waiting to provide rich memories of summer in the depths of winter.

That summer was the first time I tried growing plum tomatoes, so I was pretty ignorant of their ways. Well, those tomatoes slithered all over the ground and got so bushy that I couldn't even prune them. The plants reached out to one another, and their vines embraced in a death grip. The fruit, which lay flat on the ground, stayed yellow on the bottom and never blushed into full red. The crows (who always manage to peck away at my brightest, reddest tomato the day I plan to pick it), had a veritable field day.

So, notwithstanding the advice in my gardening bible, the next year I did what I have traditionally done with all of my other tomato plants. I gave them some support. By gently placing a wire cage around them at the time of planting and carefully placing their seedling arms to rest on the supports, I was able to receive the full bounty that my tiny plants promised. My other tomato plants stood tall next to my bushy 'Romas', lovingly tethered to their own wooden stakes. There, I could take care of their vines, prune diligently, water cautiously without creating mold, and keep the fruit out of pecking reach.

In my garden it is clear that a little support goes a long way. The many times that I have been there for a baby's first steps provide a great example for me. As a child threatens to take his first steps, my instinct is to grab hold of him and make sure he doesn't fall.

But when I just offer him my two fingers to latch on to, he proudly moves forward on his own and soon is able to provide his own support.

I've been fortunate enough to have friends who have done similar things for me. When I was starting out on my own, developing a marketing consulting business, I was terrified. I felt just like my plum tomatoes. In disarray, I slithered aimlessly about in a thousand different directions, knowing that I had the talent to make it, but unable to pull it together to grow upward. And then my closest friends came along and propped me up. My dear friend Michael gave me the most exciting and fruitful client lead that I could have hoped for. My New York friend Patty sent a dozen client leads my way. My guardian angel of a brother, Gordon, coached me relentlessly on negotiating the best deal for myself. And Bija (whose name in Sanskrit means "seed") fed me determinedly with confidence and optimism.

What I was most grateful for is that no one came

along and told me how to do it—how to run my own business, how to follow up with clients, how to create an accounting system. They all knew that I had it in me. They knew that striking out on my own was the next metamorphosis for me. It was as though long ago, they had peered behind my budding flower to see the minute shape of an entrepreneur ready to burst forth if supported properly. They staked me up, tethered me loosely, and let me grow on my own.

And it's a lesson I strive to provide to my cherished allies as well.

> When those you love dearly are struggling, don't try to control their destiny. Just provide them with a little something to lean on, and if they are meant to flourish, they will do so on their own.

"While the earth remaineth,

seedtime and harvest, and cold

and heat, and summer and

winter, and day and night

shall not cease."

THE HOLY BIBLE

RESPECT THE LIFE CYCLE REFLECTED IN THE HARVEST

10

Harvesttime is a vital starting point on a new journey and an end to an old one. Just as in life, it's important to take and to give. Know when it's time to gather your bounty and when to reinvest for next year's crops.

We may often think of harvesttime as the early fall, the time leading up to Thanksgiving when we acknowledge the abundance of the fields. The truth be known, however, each crop gets plucked when its time is right.

Ripe strawberries and the month of June are well-known partners. Zucchini, broccoli, and lettuce get harvested all summer long so that the plants can continue to produce.

If spinach is not picked at its peak, it will bolt and leave nothing. The flavor of cold-loving crops like brussels sprouts is best when the plant is nipped by the frost.

You can harvest earlier, but flavor and ripeness may not have reached their peak. Or you can delay harvesting and be disappointed by the flowering of broccoli or the bitterness of lettuce.

Harvesttime is when I see the fruits of my labor and witness the ultimate value of my preparation—literally. If I have not prepared the soil appropriately, there is the evidence, staring me straight in the eye, not providing the sustenance that I was counting on.

Gardening is something that you learn every year; you don't get it all at once. True gardening or agricultural knowledge is slowly accumulated over time. As in life, how we assimilate the lessons of our failures and successes determines how we grow and produce as individuals.

For the good gardener, the harvest is also a time of exchange. When you do harvest all of your plants, you can return the favor that the earth has given you by turning what's left of the plant back into the soil. Then the miracle known as the nitrogen cycle will take place, decomposing the crops into rich, fertile earth for next year's planting.

In life, when we violate the cycle of give-and-take, at some point our yield is diminished because we haven't learned the wisdom of sowing that which we want to reap. I've seen this breach of natural law countless times in the corporate world. All types of resources, but mostly human, are used, and with very little return on the part of the corporation.

When a company fails to return to the individual through training, empathy, career growth, and acknowledgment, the disease of our time, burnout, runs rampant. Eventually, the employee produces meagerly and at some point will leave, taking along valuable information and knowledge.

Time and time again, sole emphasis on quarterly profitability has brought organizations to their knees. Organizations that base their business on constant improvement, reinvestment of resources, and quality management, are more successful than companies that depend on faster, cheaper production. For example, our auto industry turned around only when quality became "job one."

I once heard a farmer say, "my first decision is what's best for the soil." He knew that he could take only so much without giving back before there was nothing left to take. If he didn't pay homage to the ultimate source of his fortune, a season would come when it would betray him.

Watch closely. Know when it's time to harvest what you have sown so that you can enjoy the benefits of your hard work and know when and what to give back to keep the life cycle flowing.

"In the depth of winter, I finally

learned that within me there lay

an invincible summer."

ALBERT   CAMUS

APPRECIATE THE
GROWTH OF WINTER

11

While it seems as though nothing grows in winter, the earth is truly regathering its strength, transforming organic matter into energy for next year's bounty. So winter is a time for special internal growth and nurturance, which allows you to burst with renewal into the activities of warmer weather.

The first frost of the fall summons a certain kind of melancholy. While there is plenty to harvest, gone are the days of rapid growth for most of the cold-sensitive crops. Growers of all kinds take to the fields, bringing in bushels of basil, tomatoes, beans, corn, and zucchini. The shorter, brisker days notify our bodies that change is on the horizon.

The eventual advent of winter brings with it a slow, contemplative growth for plants. The perennial vegetables withdraw much of their upper growth, and many plants go dormant. In some climates plants continue to grow underground. They spread rhizomes, root-and-shoot combinations that grow just below the surface. It's a time of stress and testing, which winnows the weak and allows the strong to survive.

Not presented with many options, plants have to grow internally, eventually producing tiny buds, which stay nestled under the skin of the branches, waiting for the sun. Below the surface of the earth, the earthworms and bacteria create organic material for next year's cycle from the past year's remaining growth.

Before I started gardening, I couldn't appreciate this passage that nature bestows upon us. I struggled through every winter, desperately missing the sun and warmth.

Then, several years back, in the fall, I became seriously ill with a virus that no doctor could pinpoint. My left leg became numb, my bladder shut down, and I developed a symptom in my spinal cord that was unique to multiple sclerosis. I was told that it could be anything from multiple sclerosis to lupus to cancer, but eventually all of that was ruled out. This all transpired around the uncertainty and eventual demise of a relationship in which I was involved. The illness and the loss rattled my soul to its core.

The symptoms persisted more than eight months and lasted through one of the most miserable winters in the history of the Northeast. I had always enjoyed enormous health, stamina, and vigor. I felt as though I had been betrayed by my God of good health and invincibility.

With no other course of action available to me through Western medicine, I turned inward for my own healing and began to meditate. In the darkness of the late afternoon, I would steer myself home through the snowbanks, assume my meditation position on the hard, wooden living-room floor and cover myself in a blanket. For the first several months, each time that I meditated, I began to cry. Sobs issued forth violently from a source I didn't know existed. At the end of each meditation, I felt cleansed, lightened of some burden I hadn't realized that I was carrying. When I finally felt no need to cry during my meditations, my physical symptoms dissipated and eventually disappeared.

During the course of the illness, I was so steeped in the horror of what was happening to me that it wasn't until much later, until well after the warmth of the summer returned, that I could appreciate the awesome growth that had transpired in my soul. Because during the most wretched moments of that winter, I had learned to look deep inside myself for my own spiritual growth and well-being.

Like the plants in my garden, I had no choice but to do some internal work. I was faced with the essential question of whether I had what it took to survive. Through my illness, I had found my center. Through my sobbing meditations, I had cleansed myself of the emotions that clouded my intuition.

And when the sun finally shone on my soul again, when I could allow love, sexuality, passion, and grace to touch me once more, I discovered that I had emerged a more resilient being than ever before. The winter of my soul helped me to find my spirit, and so I have blossomed into a self-reliant, intuitive captain of my own destiny. I have learned that I never need to look outside myself for the ultimate answers.

Just like in my garden, when it seems impossible that anything can grow and be summoned forth after the decimation of winter, up pop the strawberries refreshed by a long regathering of energy, more prosperous than ever with their beautiful white blossoms. So, too, did I come forth resplendent with more to give than I ever imagined.

Often the greatest growth takes place under the harshest of circumstances. Look deeply to learn the lessons of the coldest, most painful times, for within them lies your greatest potential for transformation.

"To every thing there is a season,

and a time to every purpose under

the heaven...a time to keep silence,

and a time to speak..."

THE HOLY BIBLE

LEARN TO APPRECIATE SILENCE

12

When there is no distraction in the garden, peace abounds. You can hear the gentle buzz of nature and be completely mindful of what is in front of you. My garden flourishes in silence and shrinks amidst distraction.

I know several people who give up their regular meditations during the summer months to spend time in the garden. There they find more silence and opportunity for mindfulness than they do with the noise of their thoughts in a darkened room.

Being in the garden is an exercise in concentration. Within minutes I am totally focused on what is going on in front of me. What needs weeding? What needs mulching? What can be harvested? Do I need to stake yet? The bees and I work in concert. The birds chatter endlessly, waiting for me to get out of the way. And the gentle hum of the hose and my irrigation system are like a mantra that bring me back to what's in front of me.

In fact, the silence that I can find in my garden is what inspired me to write this book. By watching things grow, I could turn down the noise in my brain and observe firsthand the miracle of mindfulness. The absolute cycle of birth, death, and renewal displayed itself before me, and I found that I could be completely present in a way that I never before had achieved. When my seedlings grew in the ground, I grew inside. I could allow things just to be, and with only a helping hand from me, a larger force managed the whole game.

There's a quote from Charles Darwin that encapsulates the joy of silent observation, "It is interesting to contemplate an entangled bank, clothed with many plants of many kinds, with birds singing on the bushes, with various insects flitting about, and with worms crawling through the damp earth, and to reflect that these elaborately constructed forms, so different from each other, and dependent on each other in so complex a manner, have all been produced by laws acting around us."

I have found that silence reflects a state of mind more than it reflects a physical circumstance. By taking the time to silence the thoughts in my mind, I have found that I am greatly more able to appreciate what is in front of me in the present. There have been days, months, even years that I have lost because my brain has been obsessed with controlling the future and handling the past.

Now, even when things aren't going my way, when I'm in emotional pain, when I'm worried about my financial survival, or when I think about the misery of the homeless, I strive not to fight to get out of my state. Rather, I embrace it and explore the moment, knowing that however I am feeling is the way that I should be feeling. Just like the change of weather, clouds move in, rain falls, and then, when the time is right, the sun shines and everything is clear.

> *Take the time to be silent and eliminate distraction. It is only when we are able to experience the moment that we are truly living life.*